Beauty for Ashes

Vineeta Kurien

BookLeaf
Publishing

India | USA | UK

Presentation by *BookLeaf Publishing*

Web: www.bookleafpub.com

E-mail: info@bookleafpub.com

ISBN : 9789357448550

First edition 2021

DEDICATION

To my husband without who's support, encouragement and faith in my creative ability , I would have never reached this milestone, and to my mother, my biggest inspiration, hero and confidant. This one's for you. It was from you that I developed a love for language and expression which has made this book a reality today. I love you both more than you'll ever know.

ACKNOWLEDGEMENT

To Vinu, Rachel and Hannah- for being my Rock. Your steadfast support for my endeavors is the reason I could accomplish this. Without your time, patience and sacrifice , this would not have come to fruition.

To the rest of my family -without your inspiration, teaching and support none of this would have been possible.

Above all, to the Lord Almighty- the Author and Finisher of my faith and the story of my life.

PREFACE

I have always wanted to pen down the deep yet
rich experiences life has taken me through and
put my thoughts to paper. It is not every man's
battle, it is not every man's bread. There were
definite God ordained reasons for every season
articulated in this collection. And the journey of
retrospective discovery always has and will
continue to place me at a position of awe,
thankfulness and gratitude to the Author of my
life.

The opportunity to write these poems has been a
21 day memory packed journey which has got
me inspired to further delve into greater
ventures. I am certain this is just the beginning
of many rich works of writing and I invite you to
soak this in as have I, to be transported into my
world of faith and wonder.

You fought the good fight

Just when you think life had begun, it ends
Everything you dreamt of, the world you wanted
to build, gone in moments.
Death is real, death stings
But there is Hope our Saviour brings
Grounded in the Lord,
founded in His Word
you were strong,
He was your song,
the only one who
helped you go on.
Graced. Gracious. Graceful.

Young and widowed,
sole mother of a toddler.
Life couldn't get harder
He wasn't going to be - ever around.
Never. Ever. Forever.

You weathered the storm
despite being worn
and enduring scorn

You worked hard and
saved even harder
Not once did your little girl
feel the dearth of a father
proving naysayers wrong
Beautiful. Dignified. Strong.

You said no to new love
To protect and cherish
To nurture and flourish
me, your little one
You sacrificially lived
You sacrificially loved
A great daughter, mother, sister and friend were
you
And with God your life surround.

Now as a mother myself I see
Despite all that life could have otherwise meant
to be
How honoring God with all your soul and might
Gave you the strength to fight the good fight
For years you held on
Through sorrow and pain
Heartbreak and healing
And seasons in the rain
But you left a legacy
One that will go down in generational history
Of the woman of God you were

Loving and living for God, till you took that last breath of air.

A Mother's Heart

Soft gentle eyes
Hard working hands
Feet sore and cracked from getting through life's
demands
No time for selfcare
No time to stop to rest
For she was the sole bread winner, she had to
give her best.

With a lonely child constantly needing her
attention
Rest in sight was out of the question
For even when with sore exhaustion she nodded
off
While trying to entertain her offspring,
The talking and nudging, pulling and wake up
mum calls
Would continue without ceasing.

Yet not a harsh word
Came from her mouth
Kind, soft spoken, yet stern to discipline,
She shared and taught the love of Jesus
With all of her might

She was mother and father, brother, sister and
friend
And she gave all she could be till the very end.

Daddy Dearest

You were with me from zero to three
Albeit it short, you're fondly etched in my
memory.

Kind and loving,
So gentle and soft spoken
Everyone who knew you
Respected and adored you.

A God-fearing husband, father and son
You can be compared to none
The best fit for mother
Despite all the challenges you fought to
overcome.

God has His purposes, known only to Him
Sovereign is He and faithful to the end.

But from what I remember
Your smile, your curly hair
Your gentle voice, and our times at the fair
Riding ponies, eating ice-cream
Singing songs, playing catch
While also disciplining me when I went off
track.

Brilliant and intelligent
Yet so humble and simple,
Thankyou for all you've been, for all you've
given
In the short life lived.
Most of all you gave us Jesus
A happy home, and so much love
And for everything, we can only-
Thank the Lord above.

This You've Imparted

A love for music
A love for language
Most of all, a love for Jesus.

A love for people
Genuine intentional relationships
Going the extra mile, to nurture beautiful
friendships.

A love to create
A love to learn
Embrace and cherish, and make the best of each
situation.

To be kind
To be gentle
To give it your all, never complaining what'er
befall.

In effort there is beauty
In giving time is sacrifice

All this and more, you've imparted, for this I am grateful.

Grandmother

What a special bond it is
Between grandmother and I
One that was formed
Even before the beginning of time.
I was already a part of her
While she carried my mother
The miracle and mystery of life
No-one can ever fathom.

So there it began
This God ordained bond
And of her I can say
I am extremely fond
She saw me since birth
A woman of great mirth
Loved and adored me
Always said I'm of precious worth.

She nurtured and cared for me, looked after my
every need,
Taught me and heard me out, prepared me to
succeed.
And when my world came crashing down
She stood strong and held ground,

Took me into her care
Second mother to whom none can compare
Fought to protect me, kept me safe from all
enemies
Selflessly gave,
Gave and gave.

Sacrificed her all
Never let me fall
Never skipped a prayer
Never let me lack
She always had my back.

Did her very best
Loved me till her last breath
A life full of sacrifice and selflessness
Never taking to bitterness
For all the heartbreak and hardships that were
her portion
She only praised God and gave Him all
adoration.

Grandfather

Thank you for being my father figure
I've loved watching your life
I've loved watching your love
For everyone you know, especially grandmother.

You've always held me close
I have a very special place in your heart
You have taught me so much
Life skills you did impart.

Patiently did you feed me
While I was a little child
Never a day did you miss
Blessing, and kissing me goodnight.

You took me to school, the doctor, the tutor
Protected me from a bull! taught me lessons for
the future.
We've walked many places, visited the poor
You taught me discipline, you taught me fix
things.
You've played with me, provided for all my
needs
Bought me my first bicycle and even my first
bike.

Through every fall, you've raised me to be
strong
Nursed every wound, held and prayed me
through every sickness.

The bank, the hospital, the post office, the
market
All of these precious moments of learning, never
will I forget
You've imparted in me skills, you prepared me
for the future
And when it was time, you selflessly let go to
enable me prosper.

Writing letters, remembering dates
Table manners, photography, chess, high tea and
mates
Christmas get-togethers and tinsel, we loved
playing host
Some of the fond memories, I will always
cherish and boast.

Above all, your life of prayer
Your love for all who you care
Your strong faith in the Lord, through every trial
and despair
Has taught me so much, in a life that can't
compare.

I Wish

I have wished, I was no extra ordinary girl
With a childhood not so normal,
I have wished I had just the kind of life
That a regular family had.

Dad, mom, brothers and sisters
Holidays to different places,
Uncles, aunties, cousins and more
And a lot of familiar loving faces.

I wish I was more brave
I wish I was loud,
I wish I didn't want to hide
And bury my face in a crowd.

I wish my world was bigger
I wish my world was brighter,
I wish I had pursued
My heart's desire of a career.

Though past wishes can't come true
I'm yet Grateful, Thankful, Blessed
For in the Lord my Saviour
My troubled heart can rest.

Growing up

Growing up wasn't easy
Growing up felt scary;
When as a little child, life handed curveballs
I sure did feel lonely.

I took refuge in mother
Grandparents and my heavenly Father
Somehow I made it through
Atleast in a half decent manner.

It was the Lord who kept me
The Lord who held me tight
It was the Lord who taught me
And gave me wings for flight.

Knowing Jesus

Jesus loves me
The first thing I learnt,
And the Lord is my Shepherd
The very next.

These words sunk deep into my tender heart
When as a pre-schooler, fears and nightmares
tear you apart.
I held on to this, reminding myself
That Jesus is with me and all will be well.

Although the beginning was these little words
Sunday school and church, and a house of prayer
Kept the love going, the knowledge of Him
flowing
And a passion burning.

And it is this faith, as little as a child
Who gave her heart to Jesus, to trust Him with
her life,
That held her safe, kept her rooted in Him
Coz He was so worth it, and Faithful has He
been.

Love?

Ever so unexpected,
Came love my way
When a boy I looked up to
Swayed my heart away.

Albeit with caution
And wanting things slow
I gave my heart back
As time did show.

A beautiful time of courting,
Music and life,
In time came to a halt-
Unexpected was the surprise.

A stable boat, once well anchored
Taken to the middle of an ocean and then left
stranded
Sailing back was hard, tears aplenty, a broken
heart
But rise up did I, with friends that loved and
cared.

A whole new world

Thrilled about making a future
Into the big world did I want to venture.
Overcoming challenges that seemed big as
mountains
I stood at the day my dreams would take flight.

Brave, thrilled, ambitious about adventure
Soaking in every moment, small victories gave
me pleasure
None beside me, but God before me
I courageously stepped into the plans He had for
me.

Providential care did I experience
Through unknowns, uncertainties, His hand did I
sense
He calmed every anxious thought, provided for
my every need
Took me places I couldn't imagine, Faithful
Father He was indeed!

Favor and grace
The Lord shining His face
upon me in every new phase
I couldn't be in a better place.

Building a life

You've got to study they said
To build a secure future;
I enjoyed it with all my heart
The journey of learning and adventure.

Raise my hand did I
In all I could participate
Music, debate, sport, you name it
Never once did I hesitate.

Highly motivated, positively driven
I enjoyed helping others overcome their
mountain
Building friendships, fostering relationships
In taking every opportunity, I found total bliss.

Post studying, and onto work
Providential favor and hard yards combined
Passionate to shine,
I revel in the life that is mine.

Chance encounters

It's all in the eyes they said
But when I met you, I believed
The eyes do speak volumes
And attraction at first sight, was the beginning of
our story.

You charmed me with your personality and your
looks
But soon were you lost in the crowd
I looked for you after, with little hope you would
be found.

Chance had it that at another random encounter
You would I counter
And become friends thereafter!

For a friendship that started on mountain top
Amid song and campfire,
And another chance encounter a third time
Affirmed this was God transpired.

Then did I pursue, respond, and react
From then on it was full throttle
Giving heed to no hurdle
For this boy was special,

And I wanted to know him.

Just the way you are

It's not very often
Someone captivates your heart
Someone still remains dear
After months of daily contact.

Oodles of laughter, oodles of joy
Unending fun times, this ship's sailing ahoy!
Adventures together, some quite daring
Good times and challenges, all worth
remembering.

The fondness only grew dearer
As two years together drew nearer
Growing together, praying and loving each
other,
Seeking God's will about our future.

He was my chosen man, and yes say did I
I wanted to be with him until the day I die
Then we said I do, amongst God, family and
friends
And promised to cherish each other till the very
end.

My love My life

The best years of my life
Are because of you darling,
I'm glad we found each other
To wake up to each morning.

Building a life, building a home
Chasing dreams, together we'll never walk alone
Raising a family, two and another in row
The most beautiful thing is watching us all grow.

Loving and living, through joy and through pain
Thanking the Lord at the end of each day.
Being a blessing, serving and caring
Sacrificing and giving, always sharing.

You've given me so much, taught me so much
You are a rare find, one of a kind.
I look forward to the rest of our lives
with much anticipated joy and gladness,
And despite all the other madness
I would choose no one but you, over and over
To have and to hold, always and forever.

Sisterhood

The Joy of sisterhood
Can be compared to none
Never ending laughter, cartloads of fun.
Blessed am I to have these girls
Since the years of tiny shoes and skirts.

For every milestone, every phase
There was a friend in every season
while some left without good reason,
I'm eternally thankful to those who've stuck-
Those treasures I've been blessed with.

Some sisters are forever
Sharing and growing together, Loving and
accepting each other
just for who we are.
Some are for fun times,
Some are for the hard times
While some precious friendships, are tempered
for both times.

As the years have passed
My world has become smaller
But I'm learning to stand taller
Knowing that the people who matter will stay

And if not, there's always still my God with me
all the way.

25

Motherly joys

The day that changed my life
Was when I held you in my hands the first time
I couldn't hold back tears
Tears of joy, gratitude, thankfulness.

I had a special bond with you
Even while you were being fearfully and
wonderfully knit
And as I carried you in my womb
And prayed for you since I knew about you.

Now you are here in my embrace
Closer still in my heart
And with your birth was I given
A precious piece back of what I had lost;
mother.

You will be more special to me than I can
express
My kind-hearted, loving little princess
So full of strong character, personality and life
Always ready to help, and bringing laughter and
smiles.

Failures and falls

I've always strived to live right
A promise I made as a little child
For most part of it did I abide
But somewhere along the way I did slide.

I've fallen, I've picked myself up
Dusted the dirt off, nursed the bruise, onward I
darted
For most part of it, again I fared good
But somewhere, sometime, I slipped.

I yearn to walk well
Learning from mistakes
Failures and falls happen to all
We need grace and forgiveness and the will to
move on.

Saving Love

Despite all you've been through, despite all
you've done
Somethings you're proud of, somethings you
wish could be undone
Our Father in Heaven, takes us just as we are
Loves and comforts us, binds and restores,
Truly forgives us, calls us His own.

Oh such a love where could I ever find
Nowhere but in Jesus
My greatest treasure, precious beyond measure
Is my dear Lord Jesus.
I couldn't think of a life without Him
I sure would not survive
For it is He who sustains me, helps me live this
life.

Words would not suffice
To tell of Your Sacrifice
To save and redeem me, to give me eternal life.
But with a heart full of gratitude
I want to thank you Lord for loving me
Being my safe refuge, for calling me Your own.